I Am
(Inspiring, Aspiring & Motivating)

Success Every
Moment
In The Summer!

EDWARD F. T. CHARFAUROS

Edward F.T. Charfauros

ISBN: 978-0-5784-9376-3

In Loving Memory
of

My Beloved Grandparents

Nicolasa and John Torres

&

Ramona and Jose Charfauros

Dedicated
to

My Nephew
Andrew Acfalle

Acknowledgments

Thank you very much for your unconditional love and faithful support!

Genevieve, Adrianna, &
Vernon J. T. Charfauros
(Spring Valley, CA)

Walter Dabu
(San Diego, CA/Oahu, HI)

Jason "Moonie" Mun
(Seattle, WA)

Ryan "DJ O'rion" Silverio Aguiling
(Long Beach, CA)

Christy Agahan-Ta & B. J. Ta
(Seattle, WA)

Shane Busby
(Dallas, TX)

Romy Dacaney
(Guam & Oahu, HI)

Keola Lagrimas
(Whitmore Village, HI)

The intentions of this book are for the reader to read, comprehend, memorize and positively interpret each self-communicating script daily - Two scripts per day. Each positively affecting script is meant to be used one whole day and or 24-hour period.

For example: You, as the reader will read, comprehend, memorize, and positively interpret the following script to use for one whole day and or 24-hour period.

I am success, because

I greatly continue as the day continues to greatly be, just as I continue to greatly see myself being in the future

to continue my great day!

and

You are success, because

You greatly continue as the day continues to greatly be, just as you continue to greatly see yourself being in the future

to continue your great day!

Read the affirmation scripts as many times as necessary for you to benefit and continue positively affecting your life in support of your maximum potential of true self. Additionally, this book also serves as a daily record for your goals and dreams to assist in your focus, motivation, inspiration and aspirations. I've provided additional space to encourage goal setting, note taking of ideas, progress recording, etc. Please by all means necessary completely utilize this book in its entirety, as I have intended for its use. Don't limit yourself... Enjoy these scripts as you desire however you may please yourself for self-satisfaction. If it helps, share your favorite scripts publicly, speak them out loud in front of a mirror privately, or simply empower yourself in absolute solitude as I do by repeating them throughout your day wherever you are.

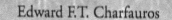

I am success because

I greatly continue as the day continues to greatly be, just as I continue to greatly see myself being in the future

to continue my great day!

You are success because

You greatly continue as the day continues to greatly be, just as you continue to greatly see yourself being in the future

to continue your great day!

My goals today to continue succeeding are:

_____

_____

_____

_____

_____

_____

_____

_____

_____

_____

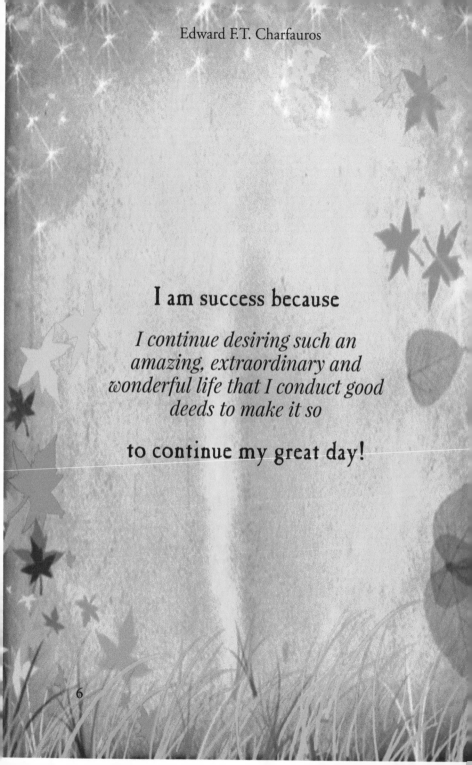

I am success because

I continue desiring such an amazing, extraordinary and wonderful life that I conduct good deeds to make it so

to continue my great day!

You are success because

You continue desiring such an amazing, extraordinary and wonderful life that you conduct good deeds to make it so

to continue your great day!

My goals today to continue succeeding are:

_____

_____

_____

_____

_____

_____

_____

_____

_____

_____

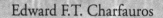

Edward F.T. Charfauros

I am success because

*I attend everywhere as a friend,
and intend to depart everywhere
just as such*

to continue my great day!

You are success because

You attend everywhere as a friend, and intend to depart everywhere just as such

to continue your great day!

My goals today to continue succeeding are:

_____

_____

_____

_____

_____

_____

_____

_____

_____

_____

_____

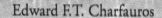

I am success because

*I have fun when I share my
services, as I love giving through
what impassions me*

to continue my great day!

You are success because

*You have fun when you share your services,
as you love giving through what impassions
you*

to continue your great day!

My goals today to continue succeeding are:

_____

_____

_____

_____

_____

_____

_____

_____

_____

_____

I am success because

*I know the best things that I ever
hear about me comes from me, for
me, to me*

to continue my great day!

You are success because

You know the best things that you ever hear about you comes from you, for you, to you

to continue your great day!

My goals today to continue succeeding are:

_____

_____

_____

_____

_____

_____

_____

_____

_____

_____

_____

I am success because

I believe my health and wealth are vitally dependent upon how great I live! By how loving I think, how positive I behave, how clean I breathe, how pure I drink, how nutritious I eat, how much I graciously give, and how long I slumber

to continue my great day!

You are success because

You believe your health and wealth are vitally dependent upon how great you live! By how loving you think, how positive you behave, how clean you breathe, how pure you drink, how nutritious you eat, how much you graciously give, and how long you slumber

to continue your great day!

My goals today to continue succeeding are:

_____

_____

_____

_____

_____

_____

_____

_____

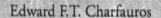

I am success because

*I continue moving as though
it matters, doing as though
everything matters, and continue
as though I matter*

to continue my great day!

You are success because

You continue moving as though it matters,
doing as though everything matters, and
continue as though you matter

to continue your great day!

My goals today to continue succeeding are:

_____

_____

_____

_____

_____

_____

_____

_____

_____

_____

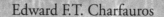

I am success because

*I enjoy being so positively high that
I don't allow anything of negative
essence to detour me*

to continue my great day!

You are success because

You enjoy being so positively high that you don't allow anything of negative essence to detour you

to continue your great day!

My goals today to continue succeeding are:

_____

_____

_____

_____

_____

_____

_____

_____

_____

_____

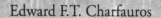

I am success because

I continue thinking with compassion; speaking with purpose; acting with passion, then slumbering with gratitude

to continue my great day!

You are success because

You continue thinking with compassion;
speaking with purpose; acting with passion,
then slumbering with gratitude

to continue your great day!

My goals today to continue succeeding are:

_____

_____

_____

_____

_____

_____

_____

_____

_____

I am success because

I am wiser to learn by people's misfortunes beyond my own, as I continue sharing my lessons with others for benefit

to continue my great day!

You are success because

You're wiser to learn by people's misfortunes beyond your own, as you continue sharing your lessons with others for benefit

to continue your great day!

My goals today to continue succeeding are:

_____

_____

_____

_____

_____

_____

_____

_____

_____

_____

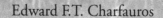

I am success because

I continue inspiring people for smile and laughter, as I inspire for better

to continue my great day!

You are success because

You're wiser to learn by people's misfortunes beyond your own, as you continue sharing your lessons with others for benefit

to continue your great day!

My goals today to continue succeeding are:

_____

_____

_____

_____

_____

_____

_____

_____

_____

_____

25

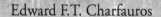

I am success because

*I am a person of loving thoughts
and a product of past thoughts for
what I think I will be I believe I am
becoming*

to continue my great day!

You are success because

You are a person of loving thoughts and a product of past thoughts for what you think you will be you believe you are becoming

to continue your great day!

My goals today to continue succeeding are:

_____

_____

_____

_____

_____

_____

_____

_____

_____

_____

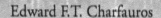

I am success because

I define myself not only through words, but through action, as I make a positive difference within my life

to continue my great day!

You are success because

You define yourself not only through words, but through action, as you make a positive difference within your life

to continue your great day!

My goals today to continue succeeding are:

_____

_____

_____

_____

_____

_____

_____

_____

_____

_____

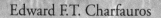

I am success because

*I continue appreciating the amazing
visions I create within my mind, as
I enthusiastically look forward to
realizing them in the flesh*

to continue my great day!

You are success because

You continue appreciating the amazing visions you create within your mind, as you enthusiastically look forward to realizing them in the flesh

to continue your great day!

My goals today to continue succeeding are:

_____

_____

_____

_____

_____

_____

_____

_____

_____

_____

I am success because

I maintain and sustain a positive mindset with the belief that it is possible to achieve positive results

to continue my great day!

You are success because

You maintain and sustain a positive mindset with the belief that it is possible to achieve positive results

to continue your great day!

My goals today to continue succeeding are:

_____

_____

_____

_____

_____

_____

_____

_____

_____

_____

I am success because

*I continue increasing my wisdom
by attaining education and
learning from experience*

to continue my great day!

You are success because

You continue increasing your wisdom by attaining education and learning from experience

to continue your great day!

My goals today to continue succeeding are:

_____

_____

_____

_____

_____

_____

_____

_____

_____

_____

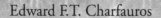

I am success because

I feel with love when thinking of my desires and supporting my imagination when attracting all that I desire

to continue my great day!

You are success because

You feel with love when thinking of your desires and supporting your imagination when attracting all that you desire

to continue your great day!

My goals today to continue succeeding are:

_____

_____

_____

_____

_____

_____

_____

_____

_____

_____

I am success because

*I continue using my creativity
for bliss and continue believing
in receiving all that I continue
conceiving with my optimistic
mentality*

to continue my great day!

You are success because

You continue using your creativity for bliss and continue believing in receiving all that you continue conceiving with your optimistic mentality

to continue your great day!

My goals today to continue succeeding are:

_____

_____

_____

_____

_____

_____

_____

_____

_____

I am success because

I remain honest with myself upon remaining to be me, as I enthusiastically accept constant change for better leading me to be a better me

to continue my great day!

You are success because

You remain honest with yourself upon remaining to be you, as you enthusiastically accept constant change for better leading yourself to be a better you

to continue your great day!

My goals today to continue succeeding are:

_____

_____

_____

_____

_____

_____

_____

_____

_____

I am success because

I continue enriching my life with love while enriching others for better

to continue my great day!

You are success because

You remain honest with yourself upon remaining to be you, as you enthusiastically accept constant change for better leading yourself to be a better you

to continue your great day!

My goals today to continue succeeding are:

_____

_____

_____

_____

_____

_____

_____

_____

_____

_____

I am success because

*I continue using myself for good
toward bettering others, as I
continue feeling blessed in thought
and making a historical difference*

to continue my great day!

You are success because

You continue using yourself for good toward bettering others, as you continue feeling blessed in thought and making a historical difference

to continue your great day!

My goals today to continue succeeding are:

_____

_____

_____

_____

_____

_____

_____

_____

_____

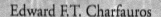

I am success because

I continue enduring through the pains and pleasures of life, as I continue strengthening my mind desirably toward being better

to continue my great day!

You are success because

You continue enduring through the pains and pleasures of life, as you continue strengthening your mind desirably toward being better

to continue your great day!

My goals today to continue succeeding are:

_____

_____

_____

_____

_____

_____

_____

_____

_____

_____

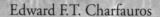

I am success because

*I continue sharing my thoughts,
whether it's through vocabulary,
action, or combining both I
continue living better by remaining
true to myself*

to continue my great day!

You are success because

You continue sharing your thoughts, whether it's through vocabulary, action, or combining both you continue living better by remaining true to yourself

to continue your great day!

My goals today to continue succeeding are:

_____

_____

_____

_____

_____

_____

_____

_____

_____

I am success because

*I continue remaining accountable
for my actions, decisions, and
thoughts, as I think optimistically
and do enthusiastically*

to continue my great day!

You are success because

You continue remaining accountable for your actions, decisions, and thoughts, as you think optimistically and do enthusiastically

to continue your great day!

My goals today to continue succeeding are:

_____

_____

_____

_____

_____

_____

_____

_____

_____

_____

I am success because

*I accept every path toward
achieving my accomplishments
regardless of outcome and result, as
I remain thankful*

to continue my great day!

You are success because

You accept every path toward achieving your accomplishments regardless of outcome and result, as you remain thankful

to continue your great day!

My goals today to continue succeeding are:

_____

_____

_____

_____

_____

_____

_____

_____

_____

_____

I am success because

*I continue self-disciplining myself
to remain on path for achieving
milestones and accomplishing goals*

to continue my great day!

You are success because

You continue self-disciplining yourself to remain on path for achieving milestones and accomplishing goals

to continue your great day!

My goals today to continue succeeding are:

_____

_____

_____

_____

_____

_____

_____

_____

_____

I am success because

I thoroughly enjoy friends and family, as I appreciate my fame among those adoring, appreciating and cherishing me

to continue my great day!

You are success because

You thoroughly enjoy friends and family, as you appreciate your fame among those adoring, appreciating and cherishing you

to continue your great day!

My goals today to continue succeeding are:

_____

_____

_____

_____

_____

_____

_____

_____

_____

57

I am success because

I inspire more smiles! Aspire more dreams! Motivate more action! Pleasure more fantasies! Bless more lives beyond prayer, words, and thought, but with results

to continue my great day!

You are success because

*You thoroughly enjoy friends and family,
as you appreciate your fame among those
adoring, appreciating and cherishing you*

to continue your great day!

My goals today to continue succeeding are:

_____

_____

_____

_____

_____

_____

_____

_____

_____

_____

_____

I am success because

I am an optimist who enjoys the best of all possible worlds beyond myself

to continue my great day!

You are success because

You are an optimist who enjoys the best of all possible worlds beyond yourself

to continue your great day!

My goals today to continue succeeding are:

_____

_____

_____

_____

_____

_____

_____

_____

_____

_____

_____

I am success because

*I continue meditating and praying
for better moments with love*

to continue my great day!

You are success because

You continue meditating and praying for better moments with love

to continue your great day!

My goals today to continue succeeding are:

_____

_____

_____

_____

_____

_____

_____

_____

_____

_____

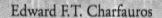

Edward F.T. Charfauros

I am success because

I continue striving with a stress-free lifestyle to continue procuring positive thinking

to continue my great day!

You are success because

You continue striving with a stress free lifestyle to continue procuring positive thinking

to continue your great day!

My goals today to continue succeeding are:

_____

_____

_____

_____

_____

_____

_____

_____

_____

_____

_____

I am success because

I continue progressing with work consistency, striving morally in assisting others for better, and remaining patient with gratitude

to continue my great day!

You are success because

You continue progressing with work consistency, striving morally in assisting others for better, and remaining patient with gratitude

to continue your great day!

My goals today to continue succeeding are:

_____

_____

_____

_____

_____

_____

_____

_____

_____

I am success because

I expend my energy creatively by positively affecting lives when possible, as I continue creating a wonderful and blessed difference

to continue my great day!

You are success because

You expend your energy creatively by positively affecting lives when possible, as you continue creating a wonderful and blessed difference

to continue your great day!

My goals today to continue succeeding are:

_____

_____

_____

_____

_____

_____

_____

_____

_____

_____

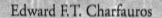

I am success because

I know I am a fortunate winner who continues enduring every challenging situation to learn from, as I only become better and stronger

to continue my great day!

You are success because

You know you are a fortunate winner who continues enduring every challenging situation to learn from, as you only become better and stronger

to continue your great day!

My goals today to continue succeeding are:

_____

_____

_____

_____

_____

_____

_____

_____

_____

I am success because

I continue adhering to my wisdom of education and experience of myself and of others for beneficial use when expediting upon my endeavors for accomplishments and achievements

to continue my great day!

You are success because

You continue adhering to your wisdom of education and experience of yourself and of others for beneficial use when expediting upon your endeavors for accomplishments and achievements

to continue your great day!

My goals today to continue succeeding are:

_____

_____

_____

_____

_____

_____

_____

_____

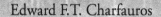

I am success because

*I continue learning from
undesirable results while focusing
on desirable outcomes, as I learn
from my results and look forward
to achieving accomplishments*

to continue my great day!

You are success because

*You continue learning from undesirable
results while focusing on desirable outcomes,
as you learn from your results and look
forward to achieving accomplishments*

to continue your great day!

My goals today to continue succeeding are:

_____

_____

_____

_____

_____

_____

_____

_____

_____

I am success because

*I continue caring of and for people
both inwardly and outwardly,
as these deeds reward me with a
wonderful feeling of good*

to continue my great day!

You are success because

You continue caring of and for people both inwardly and outwardly, as these deeds reward you with a wonderful feeling of good

to continue your great day!

My goals today to continue succeeding are:

_____

_____

_____

_____

_____

_____

_____

_____

_____

I am success because

I maintain a habit of doing what is right through self-suggestion, as I continue using the power of my subconscious mind and my imagination

to continue my great day!

You are success because

You maintain a habit of doing what is right through self-suggestion, as you continue using the power of your subconscious mind and your imagination

to continue your great day!

My goals today to continue succeeding are:

_____

_____

_____

_____

_____

_____

_____

_____

_____

I am success because

I sustain the desire to continue enriching my mind, and exercising my mentality for greatness and the better of others

to continue my great day!

You are success because

You sustain the desire to continue enriching your mind, and exercising your mentality for greatness and the better of others

to continue your great day!

My goals today to continue succeeding are:

_____

_____

_____

_____

_____

_____

_____

_____

_____

_____

I am success because

I continue communicating verbally and non-verbally with others in a positive, respectful and non-threatening manner

to continue my great day!

You are success because

You continue communicating verbally and non-verbally with others in a positive, respectful and non-threatening manner

to continue your great day!

My goals today to continue succeeding are:

_____

_____

_____

_____

_____

_____

_____

_____

_____

_____

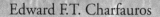

I am success because

I continue facing my fears for many beneficial and wonderful reasons, such as to learn further for preparation, alerting for safety and security, and self-awareness for better health

to continue my great day!

You are success because

You continue facing your fears for many beneficial and wonderful reasons, such as to learn further for preparation, alerting for safety and security, and self-awareness for better health

to continue your great day!

My goals today to continue succeeding are:

_____

_____

_____

_____

_____

_____

_____

_____

_____

I am success because

I do not give up or quit, but continue learning from undesirable outcomes then re-strategizing until achieving satisfactory outcomes to accomplish my goals

to continue my great day!

You are success because

You do not give up or quit, but continue learning from undesirable outcomes then re-strategizing until achieving satisfactory outcomes to accomplish your goals

to continue your great day!

My goals today to continue succeeding are:

_____

_____

_____

_____

_____

_____

_____

_____

_____

87

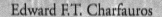

I am success because

I continue working hard smartly mentally and wisely physically, as I optimize and maximize my time and efforts for benefit

to continue my great day!

You are success because

You continue working hard smartly mentally and wisely physically, as you optimize and maximize your time and efforts for benefit

to continue your great day!

My goals today to continue succeeding are:

_____

_____

_____

_____

_____

_____

_____

_____

_____

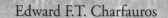

I am success because

I continue taking action upon my plans to achieve my goals after controlling my thoughts surrounding my desires, as I continue believing in myself knowing I will achieve

to continue my great day!

You are success because

You continue taking action upon your plans to achieve your goals after controlling your thoughts surrounding your desires, as you continue believing in yourself knowing you will achieve

to continue your great day!

My goals today to continue succeeding are:

_____

_____

_____

_____

_____

_____

_____

_____

_____

I am success because

I appreciate and celebrate every moment by finding the worth and value upon all that surrounds me

to continue my great day!

You are success because

You appreciate and celebrate every moment by finding the worth and value upon all that surrounds you

to continue your great day!

My goals today to continue succeeding are:

_____

_____

_____

_____

_____

_____

_____

_____

_____

_____

_____

I am success because

*I continue being happy upon doing
and endeavoring, as I love doing
all that I choose*

to continue my great day!

You are success because

You continue being happy upon doing and endeavoring, as you love doing all that you choose

to continue your great day!

My goals today to continue succeeding are:

_____

_____

_____

_____

_____

_____

_____

_____

_____

_____

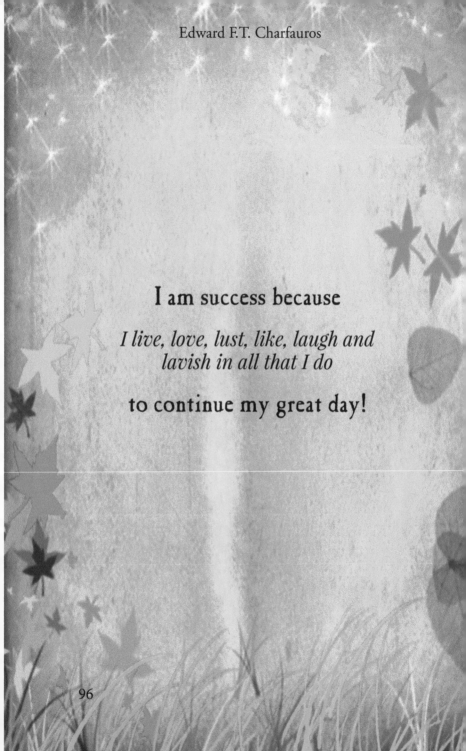

I am success because

*I live, love, lust, like, laugh and
lavish in all that I do*

to continue my great day!

You are success because

You live, love, lust, like, laugh and lavish in all that you do

to continue your great day!

My goals today to continue succeeding are:

_____

_____

_____

_____

_____

_____

_____

_____

_____

_____

I am success because

*I continue having grand, blessed
and glorious moments equating
a week, weeks equating a month,
and months equating another
phenomenal year for my history*

to continue my great day!

You are success because

You continue having grand, blessed and glorious moments equating a week, weeks equating a month, and months equating another phenomenal year for your history

to continue your great day!

My goals today to continue succeeding are:

_____

_____

_____

_____

_____

_____

_____

_____

_____

99

I am success because

*I continue to love to do all the
small things making up the grander
picture of my life, as I reflect upon
my moments with an attitude of
gratitude*

to continue my great day!

You are success because

You continue to love to do all the small things making up the grander picture of your life, as you reflect upon your moments with an attitude of gratitude

to continue your great day!

My goals today to continue succeeding are:

_____

_____

_____

_____

_____

_____

_____

_____

_____

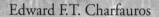

I am success because

*I continue revealing purposes
that motivate the spark within me
for action packing adventurous
endeavors, as they further inspire
my thoughts*

to continue my great day!

You are success because

You continue revealing purposes that motivate the spark within you for action packing adventurous endeavors, as they further inspire your thoughts

to continue your great day!

My goals today to continue succeeding are:

_____

_____

_____

_____

_____

_____

_____

_____

_____

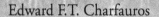

I am success because

I enjoy new friends just as I enjoy what's new with old friends, as I continue feeling blessed around them with fame and fortune

to continue my great day!

You are success because

You enjoy new friends just as you enjoy what's new with old friends, as you continue feeling blessed around them with fame and fortune

to continue your great day!

My goals today to continue succeeding are:

_____

_____

_____

_____

_____

_____

_____

_____

_____

I am success because

I continue thinking creatively, seeing lovingly, breathing peacefully, speaking appreciatively, doing positively, and proceeding confidently

to continue my great day!

You are success because

You continue thinking creatively, seeing lovingly, breathing peacefully, speaking appreciatively, doing positively, and proceeding confidently

to continue your great day!

My goals today to continue succeeding are:

_____

_____

_____

_____

_____

_____

_____

_____

_____

I am success because

I know when I am achieving desirable goals when I am surrounding myself with great people, genuine smiles, and grand opportunities

to continue my great day!

You are success because

You know when you are achieving desirable goals when you are surrounding yourself with great people, genuine smiles, and grand opportunities

to continue your great day!

My goals today to continue succeeding are:

_____

_____

_____

_____

_____

_____

_____

_____

_____

I am success because

I accept change as constant, as I continue changing my challenges for better. I know everything is temporary and no thing remains the same, as I make the best of it for a more extraordinary life

to continue my great day!

You are success because

You accept change as constant, as you continue changing your challenges for better. You know everything is temporary and no thing remains the same, as you make the best of it for a more extraordinary life

to continue your great day!

My goals today to continue succeeding are:

_____

_____

_____

_____

_____

_____

_____

_____

_____

I am success because

I convert bad challenging situations into better more ideal situations, as it is entirely up to me to go from negative to positive

to continue my great day!

You are success because

You convert bad challenging situations into better more ideal situations, as it is entirely up to you to go from negative to positive

to continue your great day!

My goals today to continue succeeding are:

_____

_____

_____

_____

_____

_____

_____

_____

_____

_____

I am success because

I continue assisting people for optimal and maximum advantage, as I know I am worthy of investment, time, quality, and the fact that I am loving, appreciative, and well thought of

to continue my great day!

You are success because

You continue assisting people for optimal and maximum advantage, as you know you are worthy of investment, time, quality, and the fact that you are loving, appreciative, and well thought of

to continue your great day!

My goals today to continue succeeding are:

_____

_____

_____

_____

_____

_____

_____

_____

_____

I am success because

*I continue sharing my
achievements and accomplishments
with others, as I fearlessly
appreciate all that exists for me for
bettering myself with others*

to continue my great day!

You are success because

You continue sharing your achievements and accomplishments with others, as you fearlessly appreciate all that exists for you for bettering yourself with others

to continue your great day!

My goals today to continue succeeding are:

_____

_____

_____

_____

_____

_____

_____

_____

_____

I am success because

I remain steadfast upon my course toward accomplishing desirable outcomes, as I reveal myself to my inspirations, my aspirations, and my motivation

to continue my great day!

You are success because

*You remain steadfast upon your course
toward accomplishing desirable outcomes,
as you reveal yourself to your inspirations,
your aspirations, and your motivation*

to continue your great day!

My goals today to continue succeeding are:

_____

_____

_____

_____

_____

_____

_____

_____

_____

I am success because

*I continue assuming the best and
preparing for the worse of every
situation both mentally and
physically, as I only expect from no
other person than of myself*

to continue my great day!

You are success because

You continue assuming the best and preparing for the worse of every situation both mentally and physically, as you only expect from no other person than of yourself

to continue your great day!

My goals today to continue succeeding are:

_____

_____

_____

_____

_____

_____

_____

_____

_____

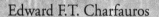

I am success because

I acknowledge rejection and failing to not exist. I affirm this, and remain patient for desirable results to reveal

to continue my great day!

You are success because

You acknowledge rejection and failing to not exist. You affirm this, and remain patient for desirable results to reveal

to continue your great day!

My goals today to continue succeeding are:

_____

_____

_____

_____

_____

_____

_____

_____

_____

_____

I am success because

*I believe with absolute affirmation
and conviction what I conceive
in mind for action I achieve and
ultimately receive*

to continue my great day!

You are success because

You believe with absolute affirmation and conviction what you conceive in mind for action you achieve and ultimately receive

to continue your great day!

My goals today to continue succeeding are:

_____

_____

_____

_____

_____

_____

_____

_____

_____

_____

I am success because

I continue appreciatively and optimistically witnessing with gratification for satisfaction all that brings joy to my life enter amusingly and gracefully

to continue my great day!

You are success because

You continue appreciatively and optimistically witnessing with gratification for satisfaction all that brings joy to your life enter amusingly and gracefully

to continue your great day!

My goals today to continue succeeding are:

_____

_____

_____

_____

_____

_____

_____

_____

_____

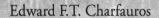

I am success because

I know it is within my attitude of gratitude to achieve supreme victory, as it encourages the winner within me to rise above adversity and overcome challenges

to continue my great day!

You are success because

You know it is within your attitude of gratitude to achieve supreme victory, as it encourages the winner within you to rise above adversity and overcome challenges

to continue your great day!

My goals today to continue succeeding are:

_____

_____

_____

_____

_____

_____

_____

_____

_____

_____

I am success because

I continue smartly serving for progress with an optimistic mindset, as I know I continue proceeding quickly to my desirable goals

to continue my great day!

You are success because

You continue smartly serving for progress with an optimistic mindset, as you know you continue proceeding quickly to your desirable goals

to continue your great day!

My goals today to continue succeeding are:

_____

_____

_____

_____

_____

_____

_____

_____

_____

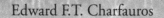

I am success because

I believe in myself, as a blessing in the flesh, a dream come true, and an example of love

to continue my great day!

You are success because

You believe in yourself, as a blessing in the flesh, a dream come true, and an example of love

to continue your great day!

My goals today to continue succeeding are:

_____

_____

_____

_____

_____

_____

_____

_____

_____

_____

I am success because

I consistently proceed with the positive perspective upon all situations by simply accepting what was, as is. Looking to constantly benefit from it all toward shaping better moments

to continue my great day!

You are success because

You consistently proceed with the positive perspective upon all situations by simply accepting what was, as is. Looking to constantly benefit from it all toward shaping better moments

to continue your great day!

My goals today to continue succeeding are:

_____

_____

_____

_____

_____

_____

_____

_____

_____

I am success because

I continue creating changes that assists me with bettering myself, as I progressively strive beyond survival for better moments, as a better person

to continue my great day!

You are success because

You continue creating changes that assists you with bettering yourself, as you progressively strive beyond survival for better moments, as a better person

to continue your great day!

My goals today to continue succeeding are:

_____

_____

_____

_____

_____

_____

_____

_____

_____

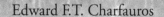

I am success because

I can't do "can't," I reject "rejection," and I fail to recognize "failing" as an option

to continue my great day!

You are success because

You can't do "can't," You reject "rejection," and you fail to recognize "failing" as an option

to continue your great day!

My goals today to continue succeeding are:

_____

_____

_____

_____

_____

_____

_____

_____

_____

I am success because

*I use people's pessimistic behavior
and negative attitudes for
motivational tools to succeed
and remind me of my blessings
surrounding me*

to continue my great day!

You are success because

You use people's pessimistic behavior and negative attitudes for motivational tools to succeed and remind you of your blessings surrounding you

to continue your great day!

My goals today to continue succeeding are:

_____

_____

_____

_____

_____

_____

_____

_____

_____

I am success because

I continue with amazing opportunities to better myself, the environment, and everyone I surround myself with through every positive action I develop and put into play

to continue my great day!

You are success because

You continue with amazing opportunities to better yourself, the environment, and everyone you surround yourself with through every positive action you develop and put into play

to continue your great day!

My goals today to continue succeeding are:

_____

_____

_____

_____

_____

_____

_____

_____

_____

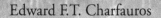

I am success because

I continue toward using every thought for being better, more loving, and feeling wonderful, as I concentrate more thought toward achieving desirable outcomes

to continue my great day!

You are success because

You continue toward using every thought for being better, more loving, and feeling wonderful, as you concentrate more thought toward achieving desirable outcomes

to continue your great day!

My goals today to continue succeeding are:

_____

_____

_____

_____

_____

_____

_____

_____

_____

I am success because

I use my core of imagination for fun, bravery of courage for protection, and support of love for trust, as I commit to an attitude of gratitude toward caring and sharing with others

to continue my great day!

You are success because

You use your core of imagination for fun, bravery of courage for protection, and support of love for trust, as you commit to an attitude of gratitude toward caring and sharing with others

to continue your great day!

My goals today to continue succeeding are:

_____

_____

_____

_____

_____

_____

_____

_____

_____

I am success because

*I know my surest way pass
undesirable outcomes and results
is by determining to accomplish,
to achieve, and to win until
satisfactory*

to continue my great day!

You are success because

You know your surest way pass undesirable outcomes and results is by determining to accomplish, to achieve, and to win until satisfactory

to continue your great day!

My goals today to continue succeeding are:

_____

_____

_____

_____

_____

_____

_____

_____

_____

149

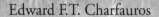

I am success because

*I continue focusing upon my
desires through my imagination,
skills, and talents as often as
possible to continue supporting my
truth*

to continue my great day!

You are success because

You continue focusing upon your desires through your imagination, skills, and talents as often as possible to continue supporting your truth

to continue your great day!

My goals today to continue succeeding are:

_____

_____

_____

_____

_____

_____

_____

_____

_____

I am success because

*I entrust in my life upon giving
me what I need and want through
vision, through belief, and through
a positive mental attitude*

to continue my great day!

You are success because

You entrust in your life upon giving you what you need and want through vision, through belief, and through a positive mental attitude

to continue your great day!

My goals today to continue succeeding are:

_____

_____

_____

_____

_____

_____

_____

_____

_____

I am success because

I continue exhibiting my invaluable principles through my actions to be positively affecting, as I continue creating a positive difference throughout my surrounding

to continue my great day!

You are success because

You continue exhibiting your invaluable principles through your actions to be positively affecting, as you continue creating a positive difference throughout your surrounding

to continue your great day!

My goals today to continue succeeding are:

_____

_____

_____

_____

_____

_____

_____

_____

_____

I am success because

I focus upon what is going well,
wonderful, and amazing

to continue my great day!

You are success because

*You focus upon what is going well,
wonderful, and amazing*

to continue your great day!

My goals today to continue succeeding are:

_____

_____

_____

_____

_____

_____

_____

_____

_____

_____

I am success because

I continue using a combination of inspiration, aspiration, motivation, action, passion, willingness, and learning from desirable and undesirable outcomes

to continue my great day!

You are success because

You continue using a combination of inspiration, aspiration, motivation, action, passion, willingness, and learning from desirable and undesirable outcomes

to continue your great day!

My goals today to continue succeeding are:

_____

_____

_____

_____

_____

_____

_____

_____

_____

I am success because

I witness the attainment of my goals many times within my mind, as I continue looking forward to realizing my desirable reality

to continue my great day!

You are success because

*You witness the attainment of your goals
many times within your mind, as you
continue looking forward to realizing your
desirable reality*

to continue your great day!

My goals today to continue succeeding are:

_____

_____

_____

_____

_____

_____

_____

_____

_____

I am success because

*I emphasize and exercise gratitude
daily to be habitual and routine, as
my daily positive changes of habit
spread among those surrounding
me*

to continue my great day!

You are success because

You emphasize and exercise gratitude daily to be habitual and routine, as your daily positive changes of habit spread among those surrounding you

to continue your great day!

My goals today to continue succeeding are:

_____

_____

_____

_____

_____

_____

_____

_____

_____

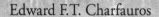

I am success because

I continue creating, thriving, envisioning, and developing with and for happiness, as I bring it forth from within myself, because I love myself

to continue my great day!

You are success because

You continue creating, thriving, envisioning, and developing with and for happiness, as you bring it forth from within yourself, because you love yourself

to continue your great day!

My goals today to continue succeeding are:

_____

_____

_____

_____

_____

_____

_____

_____

_____

165

I am success because

I continue appreciating the life I am living, as I continue enjoying the thoughts that enlightens, entertains, and pleases me to my desires

to continue my great day!

You are success because

You continue appreciating the life you are living, as you continue enjoying the thoughts that enlightens, entertains, and pleases you to your desires

to continue your great day!

My goals today to continue succeeding are:

_____

_____

_____

_____

_____

_____

_____

_____

_____

I am success because

I continue maximizing my imagination, defining my vision, expanding my knowledge, solidifying my choices, and enjoying my life by being my best through every endeavor

to continue my great day!

You are success because

You continue maximizing your imagination, defining your vision, expanding your knowledge, solidifying your choices, and enjoying your life by being your best through every endeavor

to continue your great day!

My goals today to continue succeeding are:

_____

_____

_____

_____

_____

_____

_____

_____

_____

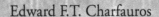

I am success because

I ponder upon past undesirable results and outcomes for educational experience, as I visualize for desirable results and outcomes repeatedly until accomplishing these goals, while succeeding expectations

to continue my great day!

You are success because

You ponder upon past undesirable results and outcomes for educational experience, as you visualize for desirable results and outcomes repeatedly until accomplishing these goals, while succeeding expectations

to continue your great day!

My goals today to continue succeeding are:

_____

_____

_____

_____

_____

_____

_____

_____

_____

I am success because

*I refuse to lose in my game of life,
because I am a winner continuing
to receive an abundance of
joyful experiences, fun-filling
amusement, awesome memories,
and loving relationships*

to continue my great day!

You are success because

*You refuse to lose in your game of life,
because you are a winner continuing to
receive an abundance of joyful experiences,
fun-filling amusement, awesome memories,
and loving relationships*

to continue your great day!

My goals today to continue succeeding are:

_____

_____

_____

_____

_____

_____

_____

_____

_____

I am success because

I continue with a positive attitude upon my endeavors, as I appreciate the desirable outcomes for satisfaction and undesirable outcomes for education

to continue my great day!

You are success because

You continue with a positive attitude upon your endeavors, as you appreciate the desirable outcomes for satisfaction and undesirable outcomes for education

to continue your great day!

My goals today to continue succeeding are:

_____

_____

_____

_____

_____

_____

_____

_____

_____

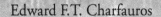

I am success because

I continue learning from my results through my positive perspective, as having a positive perspective reveals better moments to look forward to

to continue my great day!

You are success because

You continue learning from your results through your positive perspective, as having a positive perspective reveals better moments to look forward to

to continue your great day!

My goals today to continue succeeding are:

_____

_____

_____

_____

_____

_____

_____

_____

_____

I am success because

my principles are of moral value,
the same as those who achieve
greatness upon assisting and loving
others for better

to continue my great day!

You are success because

Your principles are of moral value, the same as those who achieve greatness upon assisting and loving others for better

to continue your great day!

My goals today to continue succeeding are:

_____

_____

_____

_____

_____

_____

_____

_____

_____

_____

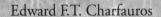

I am success because

I know what I desirably conceive within my mind is possible, as I undeniably believe to receive and achieve within my mind eventually comes into reality

to continue my great day!

You are success because

You know what you desirably conceive within your mind is possible, as you undeniably believe to receive and achieve within your mind eventually comes into reality

to continue your great day!

My goals today to continue succeeding are:

_____

_____

_____

_____

_____

_____

_____

_____

_____

I am success because

I live for loving, for learning, and for leading myself with greater purpose beyond myself; with immense passion with all that I do; and with admirable compassion with all I interact with

to continue my great day!

You are success because

You live for loving, for learning, and for leading yourself with greater purpose beyond yourself; with immense passion with all that you do; and with admirable compassion with all you interact with

to continue your great day!

My goals today to continue succeeding are:

_____

_____

_____

_____

_____

_____

_____

_____

_____

We all talk to ourselves, and yet more than half of what we say to ourselves may be negative! Life Mentor Edward Charfauros offers guidance using powerful and comprehensive communication for people such as yourself to positively affect your life for optimal long-term benefit. Assistance solving intimidating challenges, achieving goals, and encouraging a healthy lifestyle.

Featuring self-talk messages that can help you to:

- *Strengthen confidence and self-esteem*

- *Support self-growth and professional development*

- *Succeed with relationships (romance, friendships, career, etc.)*

- *Enhance healthy choices, habits, and lifestyle*

- *Cultivate respect, optimism, and faith*

- *Encourage health improvement and sustainability*

- *Enrich personal prosperity and wealth*

Use the self-talk messages inside and guide yourself for the best and ideal "YOU" have been yearning to be! Reprogram your inner dialogue with Edward Charfauros' proven self-talk scripts that assists him in taking control of his life and his destiny.

Thank yourself for making it all the way through this book! Pick up the third installment of this series of four books, so to continue positively affecting your life. Continue positively affecting yourself to positively affect your moments, your day and everyone along your way.

Book #3:

Repeat With Me:

I Am
(Inspiring, Aspiring & Motivating)
Success Every Moment In The Autumn!

I thank you for being a better version of yourself, not just for yourself, but for the rest of the world to enjoy. You, as one more person making a positive difference is one more person making the world a better place. You're leaving the world better than when you found it is an ideal situation. Until next time...

CHEERS- as your great day continues just as awesome as your great life continues.

With Love,

Edward F. T. Charfauros

186